Weather Watchers

Thunder and Lightning

Cassie Mayer

www.heinemann.co.uk/library

Visit our website to find out more information about **Heinemann Library** books.

To order:

☎ Phone 44 (0) 1865 888066
▤ Send a fax to 44 (0) 1865 314091
▥ Visit the Heinemann Bookshop at www.heinemann.co.uk/library to browse our catalogue and order online.

First published in Great Britain by Heinemann Library, Halley Court, Jordan Hill, Oxford OX2 8EJ, part of Harcourt Education. Heinemann is a registered trademark of Harcourt Education Ltd.

Editorial: Tracey Crawford, Cassie Mayer, Dan Nunn, and Sarah Chappelow
Design: Jo Hinton-Malivoire
Picture Research: Tracy Cummins, Tracey Engel, and Ruth Blair
Production: Duncan Gilbert

Originated by Chroma Graphics (Overseas) Pte. Ltd
Printed and bound in China by South China Printing Company

10 digit ISBN 0 431 18255 8
13 digit ISBN 978 0 431 18255 1

11 10 09 08 07
10 9 8 7 6 5 4 3 2 1

British Library Cataloguing in Publication Data
Mayer, Cassie
  Thunder and lightning. - (Weather watchers)
  1.Thunder - Juvenile literature 2.Lightning - Juvenile literature 3.Thunderstorms - Juvenile literature
  I.Title
  551.5'54
A full catalogue record for this book is available from the British Library.

Acknowledgements
The publishers would like to thank the following for permission to reproduce photographs: Corbis pp. **4** (cloud; sunshine, G. Schuster/zefa; rain, Anthony Redpath), **7** (Bill Ross), **8** (Jim Reed), **14** (A & J Verkaik), **16** (Layne Kennedy), **19** (Craig Aurness), **20** (John Lund); Getty Images pp. **4** (snow, Marc Wilson Photography), **5**, **6** (Vince Streano), **9** (Joe Drivas), **10** (Jim Reed), **11** (Eddie Soloway), **12** (Chad Ehlers), **13** (Kenneth Garrett), **15** (David R. Frazier), **17** (Richard Kaylin), **18**, **21** (Michael K. Nichols), **23** (lightning, Vince Streano; thunder cloud, Jim Reed).

Cover photograph reproduced with permission of Corbis (Aaron Horowitz). Back cover photograph reproduced with permission of Getty Images.

Every effort has been made to contact copyright holders of any material reproduced in this book. Any omissions will be rectified in subsequent printings if notice is given to the publishers.

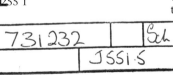

Contents

What is weather?

There are many types of weather.
Weather changes all the time.

Thunder and lightning
are types of weather.

What is lightning?

Lightning is a flash of light
in the sky during a storm.

Lightning comes from a cloud.

Lightning can strike land.

Lightning can strike water.

What is thunder?

Thunder is the sound of lightning.

You cannot see thunder, but you can hear it. It is loud when lightning is nearby.

Lightning can happen when it is warm.

Lightning can happen when it rains.

Types of lightning

Some lightning stays in a cloud.

Some lightning strikes the ground.

Some lightning strikes one place.

Some lightning strikes many places at once.

Keeping safe

Lightning can be dangerous.

Stay inside when there is lightning.

Thunder and lightning can be exciting.

Thunder and lightning show us the power of weather.

What to do in a thunderstorm

If you are inside:
- Stay away from windows
- Do not use the phone

If you are outside:
- Try to find safe shelter
- Do not stand near a tree
- Stay away from water
- Crouch down and hug your knees

Picture glossary

lightning a flash of light in the sky. Lightning comes from a cloud.

thunder the sound that lightning makes. You hear thunder after you see lightning.

Index

Notes to parents and teachers
Before reading
Talk about different weather. Ask the children which type of weather they like best. Have they ever been out in a storm? Was it exciting?

After reading
Sing the nursery rhyme: "I hear thunder" with hand actions.
Create a stormy picture on black paper with rough sea at the bottom and forked lightning striking down from grey clouds.
Play the thunder and lightning game: Divide the children into teams. Place 6 beanbags in a zigzag pattern on the hall floor. Each team member should take it in turns to be forked lightning and run down the zigzag pattern. When all team members get to the end they should drum their feet on the floor to represent thunder. The first team to finish is the winner.

Titles in the *Weather Watchers* series include:

Hardback 0 431 18258 2

Hardback 0 431 18256 6

Hardback 0 431 18257 4

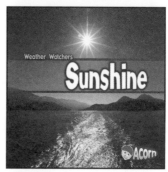

Hardback 0 431 18259 0

Hardback 0 431 18255 8

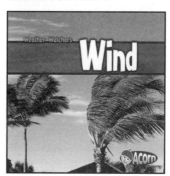

Hardback 0 431 18260 4

Find out about other titles from Heinemann Library on our website www.heinemann.co.uk/library